Tears in A Bottle

A Journey of Faith Through Sorrow and Hope in Psalm 56:8

Henry C.Ohakah

Tears in A Bottle

A Journey of Faith Through Sorrow and Hope in Psalm 56:8

Published by: Spirit Wind

Scripture quotations are from the HOLY BIBLE, NEW KING JAMES VERSION except where otherwise stated. Emphasis within scripture is the author's own.

ISBN: 979-8-322-59198-6

We want to hear from you. Please send your comments about this book to us on the contact details at the last page. Thank you.

DEDICATION

To my greatest credentials and most powerful prayer force, my best friend Anita and my three anointed children Somtochi, Chimdumebi and Chilemeze. You sacrifice daily to allow me to pursue my dreams and visions of bringing the healing world and touching a dying world.

CONTENTS

INTRODUCTION

In the sacred scriptures of the Bible, King David, a man after God's own heart, penned a profound truth in Psalm 56:8,

> "You keep track of all my sorrows. You have collected all my tears in your bottle. You have recorded each one in your book."

This verse is the inspiration for the title of this book, "Tears in a Bottle."

Tears in a Bottle is a Christian exploration of the human experience through the lens of our tears. It is a journey into the heart of what it means to be human, to feel, to cry, and to know that our tears are seen and valued by God.

The book begins with an exploration of the biblical context of Psalm 56:8. We delve into the life of King David, his trials, his triumphs, and his relationship with God. We explore the significance of tears in the Bible, from the tears of the prophets to the tears of Jesus Himself.

I have also shared a few true-life stories as I discuss this subject. Each story is a tear, a moment of human experience captured in words. Some stories are of joy, others of sorrow. Some are of triumph, others of defeat. But all are human, all are real, and all are deeply moving. These stories span cultures and continents, ages, and genders, but they all share one thing in common: they are all stories of tears.

In telling these stories, “Tears in a Bottle” does more than just narrate. It invites you, the reader, to engage, to empathize, to feel. It invites you to cry, to laugh, to reflect. It invites you to see your own tears in the tears of others, and in doing so, to realize that we are all connected, that we all share the same fundamental human experiences.

But “Tears in a Bottle” is not just about tears. It is also about the bottle. The bottle is a metaphor for the ways in which we contain our emotions, the ways in which we try to control and manage them. It is about the societal and cultural norms that dictate when, where, and how we are allowed to express our emotions. It is about the pressure to keep our tears bottled up, and the liberation that comes from letting them flow.

In essence, it pertains to the divine act of our God gathering our tears, a poignant symbol of His unyielding presence accompanying us through the manifold ebbs and flows of life. This divine companionship is a testament to His unwavering commitment to us, a beacon of hope and solace amidst the tumultuous sea of life’s challenges and uncertainties. It underscores the profound spiritual bond that we share with our Creator, a bond that remains steadfast and unbroken, even in the face of life's most daunting adversities.

In the final section of the book, we explore the power of tears. Tears have the power to heal, to cleanse, to renew. They have the power to communicate when words fail. They have the power to connect us to each other, to make us feel less alone. They have the power to change us, to help us grow, to help us become more fully human.

"Tears in a Bottle" is a celebration of tears, a tribute to their power and beauty. It is a call to embrace our tears, to let them flow freely, to recognize them for what they are: a vital part of our humanity. So come, join us on this journey. Open the bottle, let the tears flow, and discover the beauty and power of your own tears.
Welcome to "Tears in a Bottle".

Chapter One

Tears in a Bottle

This book aims to provide comfort and reassurance that our tears, whether of joy or sorrow, are precious to God. He sees each one, and they matter to Him. As you journey through this book, may you find solace in knowing that God holds your tears in His divine bottle.

Psalm 56:8, is a poignant expression of human vulnerability and divine compassion. It reads,

"You keep track of all my sorrows. You have collected all my tears in your bottle. You have recorded each one in your book." (NLT)

This verse, attributed to David, has resonated with many individuals through personal experiences. Here are two such stories:

Abi, a single mother, faced numerous challenges raising her children while working multiple jobs. The struggles were overwhelming, leading to many nights spent in tears. However, she found solace in Psalm 56:8, believing that each tear was a testament to her endurance, collected and valued by God. This belief gave her the strength to persevere through her trials.

Don, a war veteran, grappled with the loss of his comrades and the horrors of war. He was haunted by guilt and grief, often shedding tears in solitude. Discovering Psalm 56:8, he felt a profound connection with David's words. He imagined his tears being collected in a divine bottle, each one acknowledged and remembered. This image brought him comfort and hope, aiding his journey towards healing.

These stories illustrate the profound impact of Psalm 56:8 on individuals navigating life's challenges. The verse's imagery of tears in a bottle serves as a powerful reminder of divine empathy and the sanctity of human emotions. It reassures us that our struggles are seen, our tears are valued, and we are never alone in our suffering. This message of divine compassion continues to resonate with many, offering comfort and hope amidst life's storms.

It is posited that Psalm 56, a profound passage in the Bible, serves as a beacon of hope for those grappling with pain and feeling overlooked. This Psalm elucidates that every tear shed by David has been meticulously collected by God, encapsulated in a metaphorical bottle.

This intimate imagery underscores the proximity of God during our times of distress. The omnipotent entity, despite concurrently hearing millions of prayers, is cognizant of every tear that escapes our eyes.

Contemplate this profound truth: there is not a single tear that has descended from your eye that has escaped God's notice. This holds true for every stage of life:

- The burdens experienced during early childhood,
- The challenges encountered during adolescence,
- The anxieties faced in young adulthood,
- And the complexities navigated in old age.

Every burden, every moment of pain, and every instance of anxiety you have endured, God has been aware of.

Consider the life of Jesus Christ. Did he not experience loneliness? Did he not taste the bitterness of abandonment on the cross? Did he not grapple with anxiety in the garden, to the point of sweating blood? Did he not live each day amidst doubters, constantly misunderstood? Did he not mourn the loss of his friend, Lazarus?

Psalm 56 serves as a comforting reminder that no tear goes unnoticed by God, reinforcing the belief that divine empathy extends to every individual, in every circumstance.

This Psalm was probably written in the context of Psalm 34, which is believed to have been written when David fled from Saul to Philistine territory. As detailed in 1 Samuel 21:10-15, David was compelled to feign insanity before Achish, the king of Gath, when suspicions arose about him. He resorted to scribbling on the city gate doors and drooling on his beard, thereby exhibiting irrational behaviour without appearing outright mad.

The term “sorrows” in this context can also be interpreted as “wanderings”, further emphasizing David’s tumultuous journey. This is reflected in various translations of verse 8:

"You have seen me tossing and turning through the night. You have collected all my tears and preserved them in your bottle! You have recorded every one in your book."
The Living Bible (TLB)

"You've kept track of my every toss and turn through the sleepless nights, each tear entered in your ledger, each ache written in your book."
The Message (MSG)

This book aims to provide readers with a deeper understanding of this biblical passage and its relevance to self-encouragement and resilience in the face of adversity.

The Shepherd boy
The life of David, the second king of Israel, is a compelling narrative of an ordinary shepherd boy rising to the pinnacle of Israelite society. His life was marked by significant trials, remarkable triumphs, and a profound relationship with God. His psalms and songs reflected the narratives surrounding his journey - depths of David's life, his encounters with King Saul, his interactions with King Achish of Philistia, and his enduring faith in God.
David's relationship with God is a testament to the depth of faith that can exist between a human being

and the divine. It serves as an example and an inspiration for all believers. Despite his flaws and failures, David was described as a man after God's own heart because of his deep and abiding faith in God. His story proves insights that are relevant and applicable to our lives today. His faith was not merely a religious duty, but a deep-seated conviction that permeated every aspect of his life.

David's faith in God was unwavering. Even in the face of trials and tribulations, he trusted in God's sovereignty and goodness. His faith was not passive; it was active and dynamic, influencing his decisions and actions. Prayer was a vital part of David's relationship with God. He regularly communicated with God, expressing his fears, hopes, and desires. His prayers, as recorded in the Psalms, reveal a man who was deeply dependent on God. David was not a perfect man. He made mistakes and committed sins. However, when confronted with his wrongdoings, he demonstrated genuine repentance acknowledged his sins, sought God's forgiveness, and strived to make amends. David had a heart for worship. He loved to sing praises to God and even composed many songs and hymns, which are now part of the book of Psalms. His worship was not just a ritual; it was an expression of his love and reverence for God.

Many of the Psalms in the Bible are attributed to David. These Psalms give us a glimpse into David's heart and his relationship with God. They express a wide range of emotions - from joy and gratitude to despair and lament. Through these Psalms, we see a man who had a deep and intimate relationship with God.

Saul's Jealousy: A King's Fear and Downfall

King Saul's jealousy of David is a significant theme in the biblical narrative. This jealousy was rooted in David's rising popularity following his victory over Goliath. The women of Israel sang, "Saul has slain his thousands, and David his tens of thousands," causing a surge of envy in Saul.

Saul's jealousy escalated into fear as he saw David gaining favour with God and the people of Israel. He perceived David as a threat to his throne and made several attempts to kill him. For instance, he threw a spear at David while he was playing the harp and even gave his daughter Michal to David in marriage, hoping that she would be a snare to him.

However, Saul's attempts were in vain as David continued to behave wisely, increasing his favour with the people and God. Saul's jealousy not only led to his downfall but also caused a rift in his relationship with his son Jonathan, who was a close friend of David.

Escape from King Saul

Despite his loyalty and heroism, he was forced to flee from King Saul, who was intent on killing him. This marked the beginning of a challenging period in David's life, where he had to rely on his wits and faith to survive. His escape from Saul set the stage for his subsequent adventures and trials as a fugitive. It's a testament to David's resilience and faith that he was able to navigate this difficult period and eventually rise to become one of Israel's greatest kings.

David's life as a fugitive was marked by a drastic shift from his previous status as a celebrated hero. This period was fraught with struggles and hardships, as he was constantly on the run, seeking refuge in various places, and facing numerous threats to his life. Yet, it was also a time of significant growth and learning for David. He learned to rely on God's protection, to lead and inspire a group of outcasts who became his loyal followers, and to navigate complex political situations. These experiences would later prove invaluable when he became king. Despite the challenges, David's time as a fugitive ultimately shaped him into a wise and compassionate leader.

David's unwavering faith in God is a significant aspect of his life story. Despite facing dire circumstances as a fugitive, David's faith remained steadfast. He believed in God's protection and guidance, even in seemingly hopeless situations. This deep trust in God is evident in his prayers, many of which are recorded in the Psalms. These prayers often express his reliance on God, his submission to God's will, and his hope for deliverance. They serve as a testament to his enduring faith and offer profound insights into his spiritual journey. This unwavering faith played a crucial role in his survival and eventual rise to kingship and continues to inspire many today.

God's protection was a significant aspect of David's journey. Throughout his ordeal, David experienced God's protection in remarkable ways. He managed to evade Saul's soldiers and found refuge in unexpected places, attributing these instances to the hand of God in his preservation. These experiences reinforced his faith and trust in God's providence. David's story illustrates the profound belief in divine protection and guidance, which is a central theme in many biblical narratives. His life serves as a testament to the belief that even in the face of great adversity, one can find safety and security through faith in God. This belief in divine protection not only guided David through his trials but also shaped his approach to leadership and governance when he eventually became king.

David's experiences as a fugitive indeed shaped him profoundly. They taught him to rely on God, remain humble, and have compassion for the oppressed. These lessons were not only crucial for his personal growth but also influenced his rule as king.

As a fugitive, David was often in situations where his survival was uncertain, and he had to rely on God for protection and guidance. This reliance on divine intervention instilled in him a deep sense of humility and gratitude. It taught him that despite his future status as a king, he was not invincible and that his strength and wisdom came from God.

Moreover, his experiences as a fugitive, living in constant fear and uncertainty, allowed him to empathize with the oppressed. He understood what it meant to be marginalized and persecuted. This understanding translated into compassion for the oppressed when he became king, influencing his policies and his approach to governance.

David and King Achish of Gath

David's encounter with King Achish of Philistia is a significant episode in his life. As a fugitive from King Saul, David sought refuge in the land of the

Philistines, a historical adversary of Israel. This move was not just a strategic choice for survival, but it also marked a turning point in David's journey.

King Achish, seeing an opportunity to have an enemy of Saul in his court, welcomed David. David, in turn, served under King Achish, which was a surprising turn of events given the longstanding enmity between the Israelites and the Philistines.

This period in David's life further shaped his character and his understanding of leadership. Serving under a foreign king, he learned to navigate complex political landscapes, which would later prove invaluable during his own reign as king.

Moreover, his time in Philistia likely deepened his reliance on God, as he was in the heart of enemy territory. It also could have broadened his perspective on the Philistines, moving beyond the traditional enmity to a more nuanced understanding.

David's relationship with King Achish of Gath is a fascinating tale of survival and deception. When David fled from Saul, he sought refuge with Achish, the king of Gath. This was a surprising move, as Gath was one of the five city-states of the Philistines, who were enemies of Israel.

However, David's arrival in Gath was met with suspicion. The servants of Achish recognized David and remembered him from the songs of his victories: "Saul has slain his thousands, and David his tens of thousands". Fearing for his life, David decided to feign insanity. He acted like a madman, making marks on the doors of the gate and letting saliva run down his beard. King Achish, believing David to be insane, decided not to kill him.

David's time in Gath was marked by deception. He led Achish to believe that he was raiding Judean towns, while he was actually attacking the Geshurites, Girzites, and Amalekites. His deception was so successful that Achish made David his personal bodyguard.

Chapter Two

God Does Not Just Dismiss Our Pain

The divine perception of human pain and tears.
God does not merely acknowledge our pain and move on. Instead, He records it, demonstrating His role as a personal saviour who is intimate and caring. God is not oblivious to our struggles, nor is He indifferent to our pain or detached from our confusion. Whether we grapple with sin, anxiety, depression, loneliness, confusion, loss, doubt, or any other form of pain, He understands because Jesus experienced the burdens we bear (Hebrews 4:13-16).

Jesus, too, experienced loneliness, tasted abandonment on the cross, felt anxiety in the garden to the point of sweating blood, and lived day after day with people who doubted and misunderstood Him. He even wept at the loss of His friend, Lazarus. In God, we do not have a King so lofty and detached from our difficulties that He dismisses our tears with disdain. Instead, we have a King who has descended into the pain with us. We do not cry alone.

Jesus understands our circumstances more than we realize. May this Psalm serve as a gentle reminder that our pain is not unseen by the Lord: “You have collected all my tears and preserved them in your bottle! You have recorded every one in your book!”

Society often views tears as a sign of weakness, vulnerability, or defeat. We are taught from a young age that “real men don’t cry,” and are told to “get control of yourself,” “grow up,” “stop being a baby,” and “stop crying.” As a result, we often become hardened and callous. However, tears are very much a part of biblical teachings:

“My eye pours out tears to God.”
Job 16:20

“I weep with the weeping of Jazer; I drench you with my tears, O Heshbon and Elealeh.”
Isaiah 16:9

“O that my head were a spring of water, and my eyes a fountain of tears, so that I might weep day and night for the slain of my poor people.”

Jeremiah 9:1

"Cry aloud to the Lord! O wall of daughter Zion! Let tears stream down like a torrent day and night! Give yourself no rest, your eyes no respite."
Lamentations 2:18

"Every night I flood my bed with tears; I drench my couch with my weeping."
Psalm 6:6

"My tears have been my food day and night."
Psalm 42

"My eyes shed streams of tears because your law is not kept."
Psalm 119

Paul served the Lord with all humility and with tears.
Acts 20

Corinthians: Paul wrote out of much distress and anguish of heart and with many tears.

Timothy: Paul constantly remembered Timothy in his prayers, recalling his tears.

These passages remind us that tears are a natural and valid expression of emotion, even in the face of societal expectations.

Biblical Perspectives on Human Tears

The Bible offers profound insights into the significance of human tears. Two key passages shed light on this topic:

Psalm 30:5 (GNT): This verse conveys a message of hope and resilience, stating, "His anger lasts only a moment, his goodness for a lifetime. Tears may flow in the night, but joy comes in the morning." This suggests that while sorrow may be transient, God's benevolence is enduring.

1 Kings 20:5: In this passage, King Hezekiah's tears elicit a response from God, who assures him, "Return and tell Hezekiah the leader of My people, 'Thus says the Lord, the God of David your father: "I have heard your prayer, I have seen your tears; surely I will heal you. On the third day, you shall go up to the house of the Lord.""

This demonstrates that God acknowledges human suffering and offers solace and healing.

In life's darkest moments, it may seem as though God is absent. This feeling can be amplified when we face devastating storms, endure the pain of a spouse leaving, or grapple with intense loneliness. However, these biblical passages remind us that our tears are seen, our prayers are heard, and that joy can emerge from sorrow.

The Significance of Tears: A Historical and Spiritual Perspective

Despite our reputation as a stoic society, the profound sentiment expressed in Psalm 56 reveals a different perspective. David, in his dialogue with God, proclaims, "You have collected all my tears and preserved them in your bottle! You have recorded every one in your book." This statement paints a vivid picture of the value attributed to human emotions.

Historically, in ancient Egypt and Palestine, it was customary for individuals to collect their tears while mourning a loved one. These tears were stored in what was known as a 'tear bottle' and placed in the coffin or tomb of the deceased as a symbol of their devotion. Women also, while their husbands went off to battle, would collect their tears in a bottle as they prayed and interceded for their safety and victory.

A similar practice was observed during the American Civil War, where women would save their tears in tear bottles until their husbands returned from battle. These bottles served as a testament to the depth of their affection and longing.

Revelation 7 assures us that there will be no more crying in heaven. While it is comforting to know that God will one day wipe away every tear from our eyes, the psalmist reminds us that our earthly tears do not go unnoticed. God keeps a record of our struggles and sorrow; each tear we shed is collected in His bottle until the day when tears will be no more.

Consider the story of Hezekiah, who was broken and condemned, with God having already pronounced the death penalty on his life. However, Hezekiah turned his face toward God, repented of his ways, prayed, and wept bitterly. God's response was remarkable: "I have heard your prayer and seen your tears; indeed, I will heal you." This narrative suggests that our tears can profoundly move God, and His response to a tearful heart is swift.

So, what should move us to tears? What should compel us to seek God's face with the prayer of tears? These are qucstions that invite us to reflect on the depth of our emotions and the sincerity of our devotion.

The Three Instances of Jesus Weeping

There are numerous instances in the scriptures that evoke deep emotions, but I would like to focus on three specific moments where Jesus wept.

In John 11:35, the shortest verse in the bible, Jesus stands before the tomb of his friend Lazarus, surrounded by heartbreak. Despite knowing that he was about to perform a significant miracle, Jesus wept, moved by the sorrow and anguish that sin and death had caused. Lazarus, Martha, and Mary were close personal friends of Jesus, and their distress, pain, and sense of hopelessness moved him to tears. This instance serves as a reminder that each one of us is in a unique position, surrounded by people who may be in distress, in pain, or living in hopelessness. Their despair should move us to tears and drive us to our knees, pleading with God for their salvation.

In Luke 19:41-44 and Matthew 23:37, Jesus weeps over Jerusalem, lamenting the city's rejection of him. He expresses his longing to gather its people as a hen gathers her chicks under her wings, but they were not willing. This moment raises the question of whether Jesus would weep over our communities today. It prompts us to reflect on our actions and attitudes, particularly our love and compassion for one another, which Jesus highlighted as the hallmark of his disciples.

Luke 19:41-44

Now as He drew near, He saw the city and wept over it, saying, "If you had known, even you, especially in this your day, the things that make for your peace! But now they are hidden from your eyes. For days will come upon you when your enemies will build an embankment around you, surround you and close you in on every side, and level you, and your children within you, to the ground; and they will not leave in you one stone upon another, because you did not know the time of your visitation."

Matthew 23:37

O Jerusalem, Jerusalem, the one who kills the prophets and stones those who are sent to her! How often I wanted to gather your children together, as a hen gathers her chicks under her wings, but you were not willing!

He Wept for the World: Hebrews 5:7 recounts that during his time on earth, Jesus offered up prayers and petitions with loud cries and tears to the one who could save him from death. In the garden of

Gethsemane, Jesus wept for the entire world of lost and ruined human beings, his tears mingling with blood due to the intensity of his agony.

These instances of Jesus weeping serve as powerful reminders of the depth of his compassion and the breadth of his love, extending from his closest friends to his people, and ultimately, to the entire world.

In observing the current state of our world, one does not need to delve deep to witness the extent of its decline. The rampant injustice, pervasive cruelty, ongoing wars, persistent famines, and widespread suffering are all testament to this. It is a world where our fellow human beings are subjected to immense pressure and hardship.

The Apostle Paul poignantly articulates this in his writings, stating,

> "For many walk, of whom I have told you often,
> and now tell you even weeping, that they are the
> enemies of the cross of Christ: whose
> end is destruction, whose god is their belly,
> and whose glory is in their shame—who set their
> mind on earthly things."

This statement not only reflects the state of the world but also the state of our nation and our community.

The question that arises then is whether we, as a church, empathize with them. Do we shed tears for them in the hope that they too might come to know Him? Are we a church that embodies such love?

An illustrative anecdote involves a young girl who was late returning home one day. When questioned by her mother, she explained that she had stopped to help her friend Karen, whose bicycle had been damaged in a fall. "But you don't know anything about fixing bicycles," her mother responded. "I know that," the girl said. "I just stopped to help her cry."

This story underscores the concept of the 'prayer of tears.' It is about weeping with a world that is lost and hurting, mourning for a world that is broken. It serves as a reminder of the empathy and compassion that should be at the heart of our interactions with others.

The Prayer of Tears

Several years ago, I had the privilege of being invited to a weekend ministry at a church located in East London which was where Reverend William

Booth began his ministry as Methodist minister. During this programme, I chanced upon a plaque dedicated to this revered spiritual leader. I would like to recount a story associated with this individual and his esteemed organization.

The narrative unfolds during a convention organized by the Salvation Army, a time when the organization found itself grappling with unprecedented challenges. Faced with a predicament that left them at a loss for solutions, they sought the wisdom of their founder, William Booth. In a desperate bid to navigate their way out of this crisis, they communicated with him via telegram, earnestly seeking his guidance to restore their stability.

Booth responded by sending a telegram with two words, with a succinct yet profound message: "Try tears!" This advice led to a revival within the Salvation Army. It is important to note that revival is not merely a topic for discussion, preaching, or prayer. True revival only occurs when desperation sets in, and this desperation is often marked by tears and a sense of heartbreak.

This concept is encapsulated in the 'prayer of tears'. It is believed that every tear shed in prayer is collected and preserved. The divine assurance is that every prayer accompanied by tears is heard, and healing will follow.

Let us not shy away from expressing our emotions before God. Let us embrace the Prayer of Tears as a genuine expression of our faith, a testament to our reliance on God, and a demonstration of our trust in His unfailing love and mercy.

Tears, often seen as a sign of weakness or sorrow, hold a deeper significance in our spiritual lives. They are the silent language of the soul, a raw expression of our innermost feelings before God.

Tears are a form of prayer, a non-verbal communication that transcends the barrier of language and directly reaches the heart of God. They are a testament to our vulnerability, our sincerity, and our utter dependence on God's grace.

The Prayer of Tears is not a sign of lack of faith, but rather a demonstration of our humanity and our longing for divine intervention. It is a prayer that emanates from the depths of our hearts, a prayer that is as real and as raw as we are.

Remember the story of Hannah in 1 Samuel 1:10, who, in her deep anguish, prayed to the Lord, weeping bitterly. And God answered her prayer. Her tears were not a sign of weak faith, but a testament to her trust in God's power to change her circumstances.

So, when you find yourself at the end of your rope, when words fail you, remember that God understands the language of your tears. He sees, He knows, and He cares. Your tears are precious to Him, and He is near to the broken-hearted.

Chapter Three

The Divine Bottle

The sentiments expressed by David in Psalm 56:8 paint a soothing portrait of God as a compassionate caretaker who not only observes our tears but also gathers them, symbolizing His profound empathy for our deepest emotions.

Tears hold a significant place in Christian faith. They are not just a biological response, but a silent language that communicates our deepest emotions. We see this as we explore the various emotions that our tears can represent.

In the divine bottle, every tear is precious, each one a prayer that ascends to God. As we journey through this book, may you find solace in the knowledge that every tear you shed is sacred and held in God's divine bottle. This imagery is deeply embedded in the Christian faith, symbolizing God's intimate knowledge of human suffering and joy. The Divine Bottle is not just a receptacle for tears; it is a testament to the sacredness of human emotions in the eyes of the divine.

This metaphorical Divine Bottle is a powerful symbol of God's compassion and understanding. It signifies that every tear shed, whether in joy or sorrow, is seen and valued by God. It reassures believers that their emotional experiences, their trials and tribulations, their moments of exultation and despair, are all known to God. This Divine Bottle, therefore, serves as a symbol of God's unfailing love and care for humanity.
The Divine Bottle is also a reminder of the transient nature of human life, with its ups and downs, joys, and sorrows. It underscores the belief that while human beings may experience a wide range of emotions throughout their lives, God is a constant presence, always aware of their feelings and experiences.

In the following sections, we will delve deeper into the significance of the Divine Bottle, exploring its various dimensions and implications. We will examine how it symbolizes different types of tears - tears of joy, sorrow, frustration, and love - and how each type of tear adds a unique facet to the Divine Bottle. We will also discuss how the Divine Bottle serves as a symbol of God's care and concern for humanity.

As we embark on this exploration, let us remember that the Divine Bottle is more than just a metaphor. It is a symbol of the divine-human relationship, a testament to the depth and breadth of God's love for humanity. It is a reminder that every tear we shed is precious in the eyes of God, a silent prayer that is heard and cherished. So, let us proceed with reverence and curiosity, as we seek to understand the profound significance of the Divine Bottle.

The Divine Bottle: A Symbol of God's Care

The metaphor of the Divine Bottle encapsulates God's care and concern for humanity. It reassures believers that their tears, whether of joy or sorrow, are seen and valued by God. The Divine Bottle is not just a collector of tears; it is a symbol of God's promise to be with His people in all their distress as in Isaiah 63:9: -

> "In all their affliction He was afflicted, And the Angel of His Presence saved them; In His love and in His pity He redeemed them; And He bore them and carried them All the days of old."

The Divine Bottle, in its profound symbolism, represents God's care for humanity. It is a metaphorical vessel that captures the essence of divine love, compassion, and providence. God's care is often depicted as a nurturing, protective force, much like a bottle that contains and preserves its contents. The Divine Bottle, therefore, symbolizes God's protective care, preserving humanity from harm and providing sustenance for spiritual growth.

It also symbolizes God's abundant provision. Just as a bottle is filled with nourishing substances, God's care is seen in the abundance of blessings He bestows upon humanity. These blessings are not just material but also spiritual, providing nourishment for the soul. Moreover, the Divine Bottle represents God's compassion. Just as a bottle collects tears, the Divine Bottle is a symbol of God's empathy for human suffering. It signifies that God is aware of every tear shed, every pain endured, and every heartache experienced. In addition, the Divine Bottle symbolizes God's love. Love, in its divine form, is unconditional, sacrificial, and enduring. The Divine Bottle, therefore, represents the infinite capacity of God's love, a love that is poured out for humanity.

The comfort and solace it brings to believers

The connection between love, longing for God, and tears can bring immense comfort and solace to believers. This comfort stems from several aspects:
Divine Love: The experience of divine love can provide a sense of security and peace. It reassures believers of God's constant presence and care, offering comfort in times of distress.
Longing and Union: The longing for God, while often accompanied by a sense of pain or emptiness, also carries the promise of eventual union. This hope can bring solace, as believers anticipate the joy of being in God's presence.
Tears as Release: Tears, seen as an expression of deep love and longing, can be cathartic. They allow for the release of pent-up emotions, leading to a sense of relief and tranquillity.
Sense of Purpose: This spiritual journey imbues life with a sense of purpose and direction, which can be comforting. It helps believers navigate life's ups and downs with a broader perspective.
Community and Shared Experience: The shared experiences of love, longing, and tears can foster a sense of community among believers. This feeling of being understood and not alone can be a significant source of comfort.
In essence, the spiritual journey marked by love, longing for God, and tears, despite its challenges, can be a profound source of comfort and solace for believers. It offers a transformative experience that

can bring peace, purpose, and a deep sense of fulfilment.

The metaphor of the Divine Bottle, with its collection of human tears, serves as a powerful symbol in the Christian faith. It underscores the sacredness of human emotions and God's intimate involvement in the human experience. As believers navigate the joys and sorrows of life, they find comfort in the knowledge that every tear is treasured in the Divine Bottle, a testament to God's unfailing love and care.
The Divine Bottle, as a metaphorical construct, encapsulates the profound nature of God's care for humanity. It is a symbol that transcends religious and cultural boundaries, resonating with the universal human experience of divine love, compassion, and providence.
The Divine Bottle's symbolism is multifaceted, reflecting the complexity and depth of God's care. It represents God's protective care, preserving humanity from harm and providing sustenance for spiritual growth. It symbolizes God's abundant provision, reflecting the spiritual and material blessings that God bestows upon humanity. It embodies God's compassion, signifying His empathy for human suffering. And it signifies God's love, a love that is unconditional, sacrificial, and enduring.

In essence, the Divine Bottle serves as a reminder of the divine presence in our lives. It provides comfort in times of distress, hope in times of despair, and assurance in times of doubt. It reminds us of God's unending love, His abundant provision, His deep compassion, and His protective care.

Chapter Four

Tears of Joy

This chapter focuses on moments of joy that bring tears to our eyes. From the joy of salvation to the joy of God's love and grace, we explore various instances in the Bible where joy is expressed through tears.

In the Christian faith, tears are not merely physiological responses but are imbued with spiritual significance. Tears of joy, for instance, are seen as an expression of overwhelming gratitude and happiness towards God's grace and blessings. Biblical narratives, such as the joyous tears shed by the prodigal son's father or Hannah's tearful prayer of gratitude, underscore this sentiment. Imagine a mother, holding her new-born for the first time, her eyes welling up with tears of joy. Each tear, in this context, is a silent prayer of thanks, a testament to the miracle of life, collected and cherished in the Divine Bottle.

Tears of joy represent moments of overwhelming happiness, relief, or awe. They are the physical manifestation of emotions so powerful that they overflow from the heart and spill out through the eyes. In the context of the Divine Bottle, tears of joy are particularly significant.

When we shed tears of joy, we are expressing a deep sense of gratitude and appreciation for the blessings we have received. These tears are a testament to the moments of profound joy and happiness that punctuate our lives. They are the tears we shed when we witness the birth of a child, when we are reunited with a loved one, when we achieve a long-cherished goal, or when we are moved by the beauty of nature.

In the Divine Bottle, these tears of joy are preserved as a reminder of God's benevolence. They serve as a testament to the moments of grace and blessing that we have experienced in our lives. They are a tangible symbol of the joy and happiness that God has bestowed upon us.

Moreover, tears of joy also reflect our capacity for love, empathy, and compassion. Thcy are the tears we shed when we witness acts of kindness, when we see love in action, or when we are moved by the courage and resilience of others. These tears are a testament to our ability to connect with others on a deep emotional level.

In the Divine Bottle, these tears of joy are preserved as a testament to our capacity for love and empathy. They serve as a reminder of our ability to experience deep emotional connections with others. They are a tangible symbol of the love and compassion that we are capable of expressing.

Tears of joy are a profound expression of overwhelming happiness, relief, or gratitude. They are a testament to the depth of our emotions and the capacity of our hearts to experience joy so intense that it brings us to tears. In the context of the Divine Bottle, these tears can be seen as the overflow of the divine love and grace poured into our lives.

In the Bible, there are numerous instances where joy is expressed through tears:

The Joy of Salvation: The joy of salvation often brings tears to the eyes of believers. For instance, the story of the Prodigal Son (Luke 15:11-32) illustrates this joy. When the wayward son returns home, his father, overwhelmed with joy, runs to him, embraces him, and weeps. These are tears of joy, born out of the relief and happiness of seeing his lost son return home. The joy of salvation is a profound and transformative experience that often brings tears of joy to believers. It is a joy that stems from the realization of being saved from sin and reconciled with God, and it is often accompanied by a deep sense of peace and gratitude.

In this story, a wayward son who had squandered his inheritance returns home, expecting to be treated as a servant. Instead, his father, upon seeing him, is filled with compassion and runs to him, embraces him, and kisses him. The father then orders his servants to bring the best robe, a ring, and sandals for his son, and to prepare a feast to celebrate his return. The father's joy at his son's return is so overwhelming that it brings him to tears. These are tears of joy, born out of the relief and happiness of seeing his lost son return home.

This parable beautifully illustrates the joy of salvation. Just like the prodigal son, we often stray from God, lost in our sins. But when we repent and return to God, He welcomes us with open arms, forgives us, and restores us to our rightful place as His children. This realization of God's unconditional love and forgiveness often brings believers to tears of joy.

The joy of salvation is not just a one-time experience, but a continuous journey. It is a joy that sustains us through trials and tribulations, giving us hope and strength. It is a joy that transcends our circumstances, rooted in the assurance of God's love and grace. It is a testament to God's unconditional love and grace, and a powerful reminder of the hope and peace that comes from being reconciled with God. It is, indeed, a joy that is worth shedding tears over.

The Joy of God's Love and Grace: Understanding the depth of God's love and grace can also bring tears of joy.
In Luke 7:36-50, a sinful woman weeps at Jesus' feet, her tears a response to the love and forgiveness He offers. Her tears of joy are a testament to the transformative power of God's love and grace. The joy of God's love and grace is a profound and transformative experience that permeates the life of a believer. It is a joy that transcends human understanding and brings a deep sense of peace and contentment.

God's love is unconditional, boundless, and everlasting. It is a love that is not based on our worthiness or our deeds, but on His nature as a loving Father. This love is beautifully illustrated in the Bible in John 3:16:

> "For God so loved the world that he gave his one and only Son, that whoever believes in him shall not perish but have eternal life."

This verse not only speaks of God's immense love for us but also of the great lengths He went to save us.

God's grace, on the other hand, is His unmerited favour towards us. It is His act of forgiveness and mercy, despite our sins and shortcomings. Ephesians 2:8-9 says,

> "For it is by grace you have been saved, through faith - and this is not from yourselves, it is the gift of God - not by works, so that no one can boast."

This passage underscores that our salvation is not a result of our works, but a gift from God, a testament to His amazing grace.

The joy that stems from experiencing God's love and grace is unlike any other. It is a joy that brings comfort in times of sorrow, strength in times of weakness, and hope in times of despair. It is a joy that fills our hearts with gratitude and prompts us to love and serve others.

The joy of God's love and grace is a profound and transformative experience. It is a joy that transcends our circumstances and fills our lives with peace, hope, and contentment. It is, indeed, a joy that is worth celebrating every day.

The Joy of Answered Prayers: Answered prayers often bring tears of joy, as seen in the story of Hannah: -

"And she was in bitterness of soul, and prayed to the Lord and wept in anguish. Then she made a vow and said, "O Lord of hosts, if You will indeed look on the affliction of Your maidservant and remember me, and not forget Your maidservant, but will give Your maidservant a male child, then I will give him to the Lord all the days of his life, and no razor shall come upon his head." 1 Samuel 1:10-11

Hannah weeps in joy when her prayers for a child are answered. Her tears reflect her gratitude and joy at God's favour. The joy of answered prayers is a profound spiritual experience that affirms one's faith and deepens the connection with the divine. It is a joy that brings a sense of peace, gratitude, and fulfilment.

Prayer is a fundamental aspect of many religious practices. It is a means of communication with God, a way to express our needs, desires, and hopes. When these prayers are answered, it brings immense joy and satisfaction. It is a confirmation that we are heard and that our pleas have not fallen on deaf ears.

Answered prayers often come in unexpected ways. Sometimes, they may not align with our initial requests, but they always align with our highest good. This is because God, in His infinite wisdom, knows what is best for us. Therefore, even when our prayers are answered differently than we expected, there is a joy in knowing that it is for our benefit.

The joy of answered prayers also brings a sense of gratitude. It makes us appreciate the blessings we receive and helps us recognize the hand of God in our lives. It encourages us to express our thankfulness, not just for the answered prayers, but for all the blessings we have.

Moreover, answered prayers inspire us to maintain our faith, especially during challenging times. They serve as reminders of God's love and faithfulness, giving us the strength to persevere through trials and tribulations.

The joy of answered prayers is a profound and uplifting experience. It is a joy that strengthens our faith, fills our hearts with gratitude, and inspires us to live our lives with hope and positivity.

The Joy of Divine Presence: The realization of God's presence can bring tears of joy. In Genesis 46:29, Joseph weeps for joy when he is reunited with his father Jacob, interpreting their reunion as a sign of God's providence.

> "So Joseph made ready his chariot and went up to Goshen to meet his father Israel; and he presented himself to him, and fell on his neck and wept on his neck a good while."

Tears of joy are a powerful testament to the moments of divine love, grace, and providence in our lives. They are the overflow of the Divine Bottle, a symbol of the divine care that fills and overflows in our lives.

The joy of divine presence is a profound spiritual experience that transcends the boundaries of human understanding. It is a feeling of being in the presence of a higher power, a sense of connection with the divine that brings peace, comfort, and joy.

Experiencing the divine presence often brings a sense of awe and wonder. It is a realization of the grandeur and majesty of God, a recognition of His infinite power and wisdom. This realization can bring a deep sense of humility, as we understand our smallness in the grand scheme of the universe.

The joy of divine presence also brings a sense of security and peace. Knowing that God is with us, that He is always present, can bring comfort in times of distress and uncertainty. It reassures us that we are not alone, that there is a divine power watching over us, guiding us, and protecting us.

Moreover, the divine presence often brings a sense of love and acceptance. It is a feeling of being loved unconditionally, of being accepted just as we are. This love is not based on our performance or our worthiness, but on God's infinite love for us.

In addition, the joy of divine presence can lead to personal transformation. As we spend time in God's presence, we are changed. We become more like Him, our values and priorities align with His, and we begin to see the world through His eyes.

The joy of divine presence is a profound and transformative experience. It is a joy that brings peace, comfort, love, and transformation. It is a joy that deepens our faith, strengthens our relationship with God, and enriches our lives.

Chapter Five

Tears of Sorrow

Here, we discuss the tears shed in times of sorrow. We take a closer look at instances in the Bible where great men and women of faith cried out to God in their distress, and how God comforted them.

Christianity does not shy away from acknowledging human sorrow. Tears of sorrow, shed during times of loss, pain, or disappointment, are seen as a natural response to the trials of life. The Bible is replete with instances of such tears, from David's lament over Absalom to Jesus weeping over Lazarus. These tears, too, find a place in the Divine Bottle, serving as a poignant reminder of God's promise to 'wipe away every tear' (Revelation 21:4).

Tears of sorrow are the silent language of grief. They are the physical manifestation of pain, loss, and heartache. In the Divine Bottle, these tears hold a special place as they represent the trials and tribulations we face in our lives.

When we shed tears of sorrow, we are expressing our vulnerability and our humanity. These tears are a testament to the hardships we have endured, the losses we have suffered, and the disappointments we have faced. They are the tears we shed when we lose a loved one, when we face failure, or when we are confronted with the harsh realities of life.

In the Divine Bottle, these tears of sorrow are preserved as a reminder of our resilience and our capacity to endure. They serve as a testament to the strength of the human spirit in the face of adversity. They are a tangible symbol of the pain and heartache that we have overcome.

Moreover, tears of sorrow also reflect our capacity for empathy and compassion. They are the tears we shed when we witness the suffering of others, when we empathize with their pain, or when we are moved by their plight. These tears are a testament to our ability to feel deeply and to connect with others on an emotional level.

In the Divine Bottle, these tears of sorrow are preserved as a testament to our capacity for empathy and compassion. They serve as a reminder of our ability to feel deeply and to connect with others in their moments of pain and suffering. They are a tangible symbol of the empathy and compassion that we are capable of expressing.

Tears of sorrow in the Divine Bottle are a powerful symbol of our resilience, our capacity for empathy and compassion, and our shared humanity. They are a testament to the trials and tribulations we face in our lives, and they serve as a reminder of our ability to endure and to connect with others in their moments of pain and suffering. As such, they add a unique and important facet to the Divine Bottle.

Christianity's Perspective on Sorrow and Suffering
Christianity provides a unique perspective on sorrow and suffering.
In the Christian worldview, suffering is not seen as a virtue in itself, but rather a part of the human experience that can lead to spiritual growth and a deeper understanding of God's nature and purpose and an opportunity to deepen faith and reliance on Him. Suffering for Christians is not something to be sought after. It's important to remember that in heaven, there will be no more tears, pain, or sorrow.

Suffering in the Christian Context

Suffering is Not Virtuous in Itself: Unlike some philosophies and religions that may view suffering as a means of attaining spiritual merit, Christianity does not see suffering as inherently virtuous. It is not a sign of holiness or a means of gaining points with God.

Suffering Leads to Faith: However, Christianity teaches that suffering often serves a purpose in the spiritual journey of a believer. It can force individuals to turn from trust in their own resources to living by faith in God's resources. In this sense, suffering can be a catalyst for spiritual growth and a deeper relationship with God.

Suffering Was Not Part of God's Original Plan: According to Christian teachings, when God created the world, it was perfect. There was no evil, no pain, and no suffering. These negative aspects of life entered the world as a result of human disobedience, often referred to as 'The Fall'.

Suffering Has Many Faces: Christians acknowledge that suffering can take many forms - mental, physical, emotional, or spiritual. All Christians, regardless of their faithfulness or spiritual maturity, can expect to experience suffering at some point in their lives.

Response to Suffering: When faced with suffering, Christians are called to respond in a manner that reflects their faith in God. This includes patience, perseverance, prayer, and reliance on God's promises of comfort and deliverance.

The Promise of Comfort and Healing for Christians
In Christianity, the promise of comfort and healing is a central tenet, deeply rooted in the teachings of Jesus Christ and the scriptures of the Bible. This essay explores the Christian perspective on comfort and healing, and how it manifests in the lives of believers.

The promise of comfort and healing is a beacon of hope for Christians. It provides strength during times of trial and tribulation, offering a spiritual refuge. Whether through prayer, fellowship, or the scriptures, Christians find solace in their faith, secure in the promise of God's unending love and mercy.

Divine Comfort: Christians believe in God as a source of ultimate comfort. Scriptures such as 2 Corinthians 1:3-4 refer to God as the "Father of compassion and the God of all comfort."

Divine comfort, a concept deeply ingrained in Christian theology, refers to the solace and peace that believers derive from their faith in God. It is a testament to God's enduring love and mercy, providing hope and strength to believers in times of distress.

"Blessed be the God and Father of our Lord Jesus Christ, the Father of mercies and God of all comfort, who comforts us in all our tribulation, that we may be able to comfort those who are in any trouble, with the comfort with which we ourselves are comforted by God."

This passage suggests that God provides comfort to those in any kind of affliction. The comfort received from God is not a fleeting feeling but a profound experience that permeates the life of the believer, instilling a sense of peace and hope even in the face of adversity.

The Role of Divine Comfort

Divine comfort plays a crucial role in the life of a Christian. It serves as a beacon of hope during times of trials and tribulations, reminding believers of God's unfailing love and presence. It is the divine reassurance that no matter the circumstances, God is with them, providing the strength to endure and overcome. Interestingly, divine comfort is not only a personal experience but also a communal one. The comfort received from God enables Christians to comfort others who are experiencing similar difficulties. This fosters empathy and mutual support within the Christian community, strengthening the bonds of fellowship and love among its members. Divine comfort is a profound aspect of Christian faith. It is the divine solace that uplifts the spirit, strengthens faith, and fosters a sense of community among believers. It serves as a reminder of God's enduring love and mercy, providing hope and strength in times of distress. As such, divine comfort is not just a concept but a lived reality for many Christians, a testament to the transformative power of faith in God.

Healing through Faith

Healing, both physical and emotional, is often associated with faith in God's power. Miraculous healings are frequently reported in the New Testament, demonstrating Jesus' compassion and power.

Healing through faith is a profound concept in Christianity. It is the belief that faith in God and Jesus Christ can bring about physical, emotional, and spiritual healing. It encompasses the power of prayer, the role of the Holy Spirit, the support of the Christian community, and the belief in God as the ultimate healer. While faith healing does not negate the importance of medical treatment, it provides a spiritual dimension to the healing process, offering hope, comfort, and strength to those in need.

Faith and Miracles

The New Testament contains numerous accounts of Jesus healing the sick, showcasing the power of faith. These miracles serve as a testament to the belief that faith can lead to healing. Here are just a few examples.

Healing a Centurion's Servant: In Matthew 8:5-13 and Luke 7:1-10, Jesus heals a centurion's servant who was paralyzed and suffering.

Healing a Paralytic: In Matthew 9:1-8, Mark 2:1-12, and Luke 5:17-26, Jesus heals a paralytic man whose friends lowered him through the roof of a house to reach Jesus.

Healing a Woman with a Bleeding Disorder: In Matthew 9:20-22, Mark 5:25-34, and Luke 8:43-48, Jesus heals a woman who had been bleeding for twelve years.

Healing Two Blind Men: In Matthew 9:27-31, Jesus heals two blind men who followed him, calling out for mercy.

Healing a Man with a Withered Hand: In Matthew 12:9-14, Mark 3:1-6, and Luke 6:6-11, Jesus heals a man with a withered hand on the Sabbath.

These accounts demonstrate Jesus' compassion and power, providing hope and healing to those in need.

Prayer and Healing

Prayer is a fundamental aspect of faith healing in Christianity. Christians believe that prayer can invoke God's healing power. The act of praying can provide comfort, peace, and a sense of connection with God. Also, the Holy Spirit plays a crucial role in healing. The Holy Spirit is seen as a helper and comforter, providing strength and support in times of illness and recovery.

The church community plays a significant role in faith healing. The church provides a supportive environment where believers can gather to pray and seek healing. This sense of community can be a powerful aid in the healing process. But God is the ultimate Healer. He is the ultimate source of healing. Christians believe that all healing comes from God, whether it is physical healing or the inner healing of the spirit.

Spiritual comfort is found in the promise of eternal life through Jesus Christ. The healing of the spirit involves repentance, forgiveness of sins, and the transformative power of the Holy Spirit.

Indeed, spiritual comfort and healing are significant aspects of Christian faith. The promise of eternal life through Jesus Christ provides believers with a profound sense of hope and comfort. This belief asserts that despite the challenges and sufferings in this earthly life, there is the assurance of a blissful, eternal life in the presence of God.

The healing of thc spirit is another crucial aspect. It involves repentance, which is the recognition and confession of one's sins, and seeking God's forgiveness. This process is often accompanied by a transformative experience brought about by the Holy Spirit. The Holy Spirit guides all believers in their spiritual journey, helping them grow in faith, love, and holiness.

These elements together contribute to the spiritual well-being of individuals, providing them with peace, comfort, and a sense of purpose in life. They form the core of the Christian faith and are instrumental in shaping the believers' worldview and actions.

The promise of comfort and healing is multifaceted. These are brought about through Prayer. Prayer is a powerful tool for seeking comfort and healing. As Christians we believe that God hears us when we pray, and He responds with love and mercy.

Furthermore, the Bible offers countless verses that provide comfort and promise healing. These scriptures are often turned to during times of need.

The life, death, and resurrection of Jesus Christ is the ultimate promise of comfort and healing for Christians. Through Him, believers find peace, hope, and the promise of eternal life.

Tears of sorrow are a universal human experience, and the Bible is replete with instances where men and women of faith have cried out to God in their distress. These instances serve as powerful reminders of the human capacity for sorrow, but also of God's unending comfort and mercy.

David: Known as a man after God's own heart, David often expressed his sorrow through psalms. In Psalm 6:6, he says,

"I am weary with my moaning; every night I flood my bed with tears; I drench my couch with my weeping."

Yet, David always found comfort in God's presence, expressing trust in God's deliverance. Indeed, David's relationship with God in the Bible is a profound example of faith and reliance on divine comfort in times of sorrow. Despite his trials and tribulations, David found solace in his faith, turning his sorrow into prayers and psalms. His expressions of grief are deeply human, yet his enduring faith offers a powerful testament to God's comforting presence in times of distress. We can learn a lot about David's experiences, exploring how his tears of sorrow were transformed into expressions of faith and trust in God's deliverance.

Hannah's story is another powerful testament to faith in the face of despair. Stricken with the sorrow of childlessness, Hannah turned to God in her anguish, her prayers marked by bitter weeping. Yet, in her despair, she never lost faith. Her prayers were heard, and she was blessed with a son, Samuel, who would grow up to be a great prophet. This narrative underscores the theme of sorrow transformed through faith and the power of prayer. It highlights that even in the depths of despair, faith can lead to miraculous outcomes. Hannah's story, like David's, offers a profound lesson about the power of faith and the comfort and deliverance that can come from God.

In her deep anguish, she prayed to the Lord, weeping bitterly because of her childlessness. God heard her prayer, and she eventually gave birth to Samuel, who became a great prophet.

"And she was in bitterness of soul, and prayed to the Lord and wept in anguish."
1 Samuel 1:10

Jesus

Even Jesus wept in times of sorrow. In John 11:35, upon the death of his friend Lazarus, Jesus wept openly. This instance reminds us that sorrow is a part of the human experience, and even the Son of God was not exempt from it. It is a powerful testament to the depth of Jesus' compassion and his shared experience of human sorrow.

This shortest verse in the Bible, "Jesus wept," reveals a profound truth: that grief and sorrow are integral parts of the human condition, and even Jesus, the Son of God, was not immune to such feelings. His tears were a demonstration of his deep love for Lazarus and his empathy for all those who grieve. This narrative reminds us that it's okay to express our sorrow and grief openly, and that we are not alone in our suffering. Just as Hannah's faith was rewarded in her time of sorrow, Jesus' sorrow was also transformed with the resurrection of Lazarus, offering hope and comfort in times of despair. These stories collectively highlight the transformative power of faith and prayer in overcoming sorrow.

After denying Jesus three times, Peter "wept bitterly" (Luke 22:62). Despite his deep regret and sorrow, Peter was forgiven and went on to play a crucial role in the early Christian church.

Peter's story is a powerful testament to the concept of redemption and forgiveness in Christian theology. Despite his initial denial of Jesus during a critical moment, Peter's sincere repentance led to his forgiveness. This event served as a turning point, after which Peter became one of the most influential figures in the early Christian church. His journey underscores the Christian belief in the possibility of redemption and the transformative power of faith.

These instances remind us that it's okay to express our sorrow and cry out to God in our distress. They also reassure us that God hears our cries and provides comfort in our times of sorrow. As Psalm 34:18 says,

"The Lord is close to the broken-hearted and saves those who are crushed in spirit.

Chapter Six
Tears of Frustration

In this chapter, we explore the tears that come from frustration. We examine biblical characters who experienced frustration and how they turned to God for strength and guidance. Tears of frustration are a universal human experience, a silent language that communicates our inner turmoil when words fail us. They are the body's response to the overwhelming feelings of disappointment, helplessness, and exasperation that frustration brings.

Frustration arises when our efforts to reach a goal are thwarted. It could be a minor inconvenience, like a traffic jam when you're running late, or a significant setback, like repeated rejections in job applications. Regardless of the cause, the effect is the same - a sense of powerlessness that manifests in tears.

These tears, however, are not a sign of weakness. Instead, they are a testament to our determination and resilience. They signify our refusal to be complacent, our desire to strive for better, and our disappointment when reality falls short of our expectations.

Moreover, tears of frustration can be cathartic. They allow us to vent our pent-up emotions, providing a release for the stress and tension built up inside us. Crying can reset our emotional equilibrium, helping us regain our composure and approach the problem with a fresh perspective.

However, while it's essential to acknowledge and express our feelings, it's equally important not to dwell on them. Tears of frustration should be a catalyst for change, prompting us to reassess our situation, identify the obstacles in our path, and devise a new strategy to overcome them.

Tears of frustration, while painful, are a part of our emotional repertoire. They reflect our passion, our ambition, and our humanity. So, the next time you find yourself shedding tears of frustration, remember - it's okay. It's a sign that you care, that you're striving, and most importantly, that you're human.

Life's challenges often lead to tears of frustration. In such moments, the Christian faith offers solace, encouraging believers to cast their anxieties on God. The story of Job, who, despite his frustrations and sufferings, remained steadfast in his faith, serves as a powerful example. These tears of frustration, too, are collected in the Divine Bottle, symbolizing God's understanding, and acceptance of human.

Tears of frustration are a universal symbol of the struggles we face when our efforts seem in vain, when our goals seem unreachable, and when our dreams seem unattainable. In the Divine Bottle, these tears hold a significant place as they represent the challenges we face in our pursuit of our aspirations.

When we shed tears of frustration, we are expressing our disappointment, our disillusionment, and our despair. These tears are a testament to the obstacles we have encountered, the setbacks we have experienced, and the hurdles we have had to overcome. They are the tears we shed when we face rejection, when we encounter failure, or when we are confronted with the harsh realities of our limitations.

In the Divine Bottle, these tears of frustration are preserved as a reminder of our perseverance and our determination. They serve as a testament to the strength of our resolve in the face of adversity. They are a tangible symbol of the challenges we have faced and the efforts we have made to overcome them.

Moreover, tears of frustration also reflect our capacity for resilience and tenacity. They are the tears we shed when we refuse to give up, when we persist in the face of adversity, or when we are determined to overcome our limitations. These tears are a testament to our ability to persevere and to persist in the face of adversity.

Understanding tears of frustration in the light of faith

In the light of faith, tears of frustration can be seen as a form of emotional release and a call for divine intervention. They are an expression of our human vulnerability and a testament to the trials we face in life.

From a Christian perspective, these tears can be understood as a form of prayer, a non-verbal communication with God expressing our innermost feelings of frustration and helplessness. They are a plea for comfort, strength, and guidance in times of distress. God is aware of our struggles and is with us in our pain.

In the face of frustration, faith provides hope. It assures us that our trials are temporary, and that God is with us, providing comfort and healing. The transformative power of the Holy Spirit helps us to find peace amidst our struggles and fosters resilience within us.

In the light of faith, tears of frustration are a bridge to divine connection. They are a part of our spiritual journey, leading us towards growth, healing, and a deeper relationship with God.

Biblical Guidance for Times of Confusion and Frustration

In the face of confusion and frustration, we should seek solace and guidance in our faith. The Bible, as a cornerstone of Christian faith, offers profound wisdom and guidance for these challenging times. Its teachings encourage patience, understanding, trust in God, and submission to His will. By turning to these biblical teachings in challenging times, believers can find comfort, guidance, and a renewed sense of hope.

Learning from Jesus

Jesus Christ, our Master and perfect example, provides a model of patience, resilience, and faith in the face of adversity. His teachings and actions, as recorded in the New Testament, offer valuable lessons for dealing with confusion and frustration. One of my favourite places in the Bible is Proverbs 24:16. It states,

"For a righteous man may fall seven times And rise again, But the wicked shall fall by calamity."

This verse encourages believers to persevere through difficulties, drawing strength from their faith in God.

One of the most fundamental teachings of the Bible is to trust in God. Proverbs 3:5-6 encourages believers to rely on God's wisdom and guidance, especially when faced with confusion or frustration. It reassures that God's plan, though it may not always be clear, is ultimately for the good.

"Trust in the Lord with all your heart, And lean not on your own understanding; In all your ways acknowledge Him, And He shall direct your paths."

The Bible places great emphasis on the virtues of patience and understanding.

"Whoever is patient has great understanding, but one who is quick-tempered displays folly."
Proverbs 14:29(NIV)

This verse underscores the importance of patience in gaining understanding and managing frustrations.

In times of confusion and frustration, the Bible encourages believers to wait patiently for the Lord. Psalm 40:1 reassures us that God hears our prayers and will respond in His perfect timing.

"I waited patiently for the Lord; he turned to me and heard my cry."

Submission to God

The Bible teaches that while humans can make plans, it is ultimately God's purpose that prevails. Proverbs 19:21 says,

"You can make many plans, but the Lord's purpose will prevail."

This verse encourages believers to submit their plans to God, trusting that His purpose will prevail even when their plans fail.

James 1:19-20 encourages believers to manage their frustrations by being quick to listen and slow to react in anger.

"Everyone should be quick to listen, slow to speak and slow to become angry because human anger does not produce the righteousness that God desires."

The Role of Prayer and Trust in God During Challenging Times

Prayer and trust in God play a vital role during challenging times. They provide comfort, strength, and guidance, helping individuals navigate their difficulties with grace and resilience. By fostering a deep sense of connection with God and a firm belief in His wisdom and plan, prayer and trust can serve as powerful tools for overcoming adversity and finding peace amidst chaos. In times of adversity, I've always learnt to turn to my faith in Christ for comfort and guidance. Central to this faith is the practice of prayer and the trust in God's wisdom and benevolence. Prayer, in its essence, is a form of communication with God. It provides a platform for expressing emotions, seeking guidance, and finding solace. During challenging times, prayer can serve as a source of comfort and strength. It allows us to voice our fears, frustrations, and hopes, fostering a sense of peace and acceptance. As stated in Philippians 4:6-7,

"Do not be anxious about anything, but in every situation, by prayer and petition, with thanksgiving, present your requests to God. And the peace of God, which transcends all understanding, will guard your hearts and your minds in Christ Jesus."

Trust in God is a fundamental aspect of faith. It involves believing in God's wisdom, love, and plan, even when circumstances are challenging, and the future seems uncertain. Proverbs 3:5-6 underscores the importance of trusting in God's wisdom and plan, especially during challenging times.

"Trust in the Lord with all your heart and lean not on your own understanding; in all your ways submit to him, and he will make your paths straight."

Prayer and trust in God can play a crucial role in overcoming challenges. Through prayer, individuals can find the strength and courage to face their difficulties. Trust in God, on the other hand, can provide a sense of hope and assurance that these challenges are part of a larger plan and will ultimately lead to growth and understanding. As stated in Romans 8:28, "And we know that in all things God works for the good of those who love him, who have been called according to his purpose."

Chapter Seven
Tears of Love

There are some tears shed out of love. We explore the depth of God's love for us and how understanding this love often brings us to tears.

Tears shed out of love for God and others hold a special place in the Christian faith. The Bible recounts several instances of such tears, from Mary Magdalene washing Jesus' feet with her tears to Paul's tearful farewells. These tears of love, shed in moments of deep spiritual connection and empathy, are treasured in the divine bottle.

Tears of love are a profound symbol of the depth and intensity of human emotions. They represent the joy and sorrow, the longing and fulfilment, the ecstasy and agony that love can bring.

When we shed tears of love, we are expressing our deepest emotions. These tears can be a sign of our joy at finding love, our sorrow at losing it, or our longing for it. They can be tears of happiness shed at a wedding, tears of sorrow shed at a farewell, or tears of longing shed in solitude.

These tears of love are preserved as a testament to the power of love. They serve as a reminder of the joy and sorrow, the longing and fulfilment, the ecstasy and agony that love can bring. They are a tangible symbol of the depth and intensity of our emotions and compassion that we are capable of expressing.

Moreover, tears of love also reflect our capacity for empathy and compassion. They are the tears we shed when we feel the pain of others, when we share their joy, or when we empathize with their sorrow. These tears are a testament to our ability to connect with others on a deep emotional level.

Tears are an expression of deep love for God and fellow human beings. Tears shed during prayer and worship are often seen as a sign of a deep, personal relationship with God. They are an expression of love, awe, and reverence for the divine. These tears, often referred to as "tears of joy" or "spiritual tears," are believed to cleanse the soul and bring the individual closer to God. They are a testament to the overwhelming love and awe that one feels in the presence of God's greatness and mercy.

As Christians we follow the teachings and example of our Lord and Saviour Jesus Christ, who showed immense love and compassion for others. Tears shed out of love for others are seen as a reflection of Christ's love. They are a response to the pain and suffering of others and a manifestation of the commandment to "love thy neighbour." These tears are a testament to the empathy and compassion that Christians are called to show towards others.

Tears are often seen as a form of prayer. They are a silent plea for healing, not just for oneself, but also for others. When shed out of love for those who are suffering, these tears become a powerful prayer for their healing and well-being.

As we have seen, tears shed out of love for God and others hold a deep significance in the Christian tradition. They are a powerful expression of love, empathy, and compassion. They reflect the teachings of Jesus Christ and the Christian call to love and serve others. So, the next time you find yourself shedding tears out of love, remember their significance and embrace them as a testament to your faith and your capacity for love and compassion.

Instances from the Bible Showcasing Tears of Love
The Bible, as a rich tapestry of human experiences and divine interactions, presents numerous instances where tears are shed out of deep love. These instances underscore the profound emotional depth of biblical characters and their relationships with God and each other.

Jesus Weeping Over Jerusalem (Luke 19:41-44): Jesus, moved by His love for the city and its people, wept over Jerusalem. His tears were an expression of His deep sorrow for the city's impending destruction and the suffering its people would endure.

Mary Magdalene at the Tomb (John 20:11-18): Mary Magdalene, in her deep love for Jesus, wept at His tomb after His crucifixion. Her tears were a testament to her profound grief and love for her Lord.

David's Lament for Jonathan (2 Samuel 1:11-12): King David wept for his friend Jonathan after learning about his death. His tears were an expression of his deep love and friendship for Jonathan.

Peter's Tears of Repentance (Luke 22:62): Peter, realizing that he had denied Jesus three times just as Jesus had predicted, wept bitterly. His tears were a sign of his deep love for Jesus and his sorrow for his own actions.

The Woman Who Anointed Jesus' Feet (Luke 7:36-50): A woman, in her love and gratitude for Jesus, wept and used her tears to wash His feet. Her tears were a symbol of her love for Jesus and her gratitude for His forgiveness.

These instances from the Bible highlight the depth of love that can move individuals to tears. They serve as powerful reminders of the capacity for love and compassion inherent in the human spirit. Whether it is love for God, love for a friend, or love born out of gratitude, these tears bear testimony to the profound emotional experiences that such love can evoke.

The Connection Between Love, Longing for God, and Tears

The interplay between love, longing for God, and tears is a profound theme that resonates across various religious and spiritual traditions. This connection is often depicted as a deeply personal and transformative experience that shapes one's spiritual journey.

Love, in its purest form, is often seen as the foundation of one's relationship with God. This love is not merely an emotion but a state of being that transcends the physical realm. It is a divine love that seeks unity with God and is willing to endure trials and tribulations in its pursuit.

The longing for God is a natural consequence of this divine love. It is a deep yearning to be closer to God, to understand His ways, and to be in His presence. This longing is often described as a thirst or hunger that can only be quenched by God Himself.

Tears often serve as a powerful expression of this love and longing. They are seen as the soul's language, a raw and unfiltered expression of the heart's deepest desires. Tears can be a response to the overwhelming love one feels for God, the pain of separation, or the joy of experiencing His presence.

The connection between love, longing for God, and tears is a testament to the depth and intensity of the spiritual journey. It underscores the transformative power of love and longing, and the role of tears as a cathartic expression of these deep-seated emotions. This connection serves as a reminder of the profound ways in which our emotional and spiritual lives are intertwined.

Chapter Eight
Every Tear Matters

In the concluding chapter, we affirm that every tear is significant to God. We discuss how God values our emotions and is with us in every circumstance, collecting each tear we shed in His divine bottle.

In this chapter, we delve into the profound truth that every tear we shed is significant to God. Our tears, whether of joy, sorrow, frustration, or triumph, are never unnoticed by Him. They are a testament to our human experience, and each one holds a special place in His divine understanding.

God values our emotions. He created us with the capacity to feel deeply, and these feelings are not trivial to Him. Every burst of laughter, every sigh of relief, every gasp of surprise, and every tear of frustration is precious in His sight. He understands our emotions, not just as responses to our circumstances, but as reflections of our hearts. Moreover, God is with us in every circumstance. In times of joy, He rejoices with us. In times of sorrow, He comforts us. In times of frustration, He provides us with patience. And in times of fear, He offers us courage. He is not a distant observer but an intimate companion who shares in our every experience.

When David speaks of God collecting our tears in His bottle, he beautifully illustrates how God cherishes our emotions. Just as we would collect precious items in a bottle, God collects each tear we shed. Every tear is a testament to our experiences, our challenges, our victories, and our growth. And God, in His infinite love, values each one.
Every tear matters to God. Our tears of frustration, along with all our other emotions, are significant. They are seen, they are valued, and they are cherished by God. So, the next time you shed a tear, remember - it does not go unnoticed. It is collected and treasured by God, a silent reminder of His constant presence and unfailing love.

The Intriguing World of Tears

Tears, a common yet fascinating aspect of human life, are often associated with emotional states such as joy, sadness, or pain. However, they serve a multitude of functions beyond the realm of emotions.

Types of Tears

Human eyes produce three different kinds of tears: basal tears, reflex tears, and emotional tears.

- Basal tears are present in our eyes all the time to lubricate, nourish, and protect the cornea.
- Reflex tears are formed when our eyes need to wash away harmful irritants, such as smoke or onion fumes.
- Emotional tears are produced in response to various emotional states.

Composition of Tears

Tears are not merely saline. They are composed of enzymes, electrolytes, metabolites, and lipids. Each tear has three layers: An inner mucus layer that keeps the tear attached to the eye; A watery middle layer to keep the eye hydrated, repel bacteria, and protect the cornea; An outer oily layer to keep the surface of the tear smooth for the eye to see through, and to prevent the other layers from evaporating.

Tears are created by the lacrimal glands located above each eye and are dispersed across the eye's surface by blinking. They are drained by tiny holes in the corners of the eyelids, funnelled into the nose, and either evaporate or are reabsorbed.

Emotional tears, produced in response to joy, sadness, fear, and other emotional states, are a uniquely human phenomenon. Some scientists hypothesize that emotional tears contain additional hormones and proteins not present in basal or reflex tears.

Tears and Gender
Studies report that women cry at least twice as much as men. Men's tear ducts are larger than women's, meaning that when men cry, their tears are less likely to spill down their faces.

Tears and Age
Basal tear production slows with age, leading to the development of dry eye, a common problem for people undergoing hormonal changes, especially women during pregnancy and menopause.

Tears and Onions
Chopping onions causes tears because it releases syn-Propanethial S-oxide, an irritant that affects the lacrimal gland.

Tears and Stress

Some scientists believe that emotional tears contain stress hormones, so crying makes a person feel better by purging some of the negative stress.

Tears are a fascinating aspect of human physiology, serving a multitude of functions beyond the realm of emotions. They are essential for maintaining the health of our eyes, communicating our emotions, and even helping us cope with stress.

But perhaps the most poignant aspect of tears is their role as a call for comfort. When we cry, we expose our vulnerability, implicitly reaching out to others for support. Tears can bridge the gap between individuals, breaking down walls and fostering a sense of shared experience. They remind us of our inherent need for others, our desire for empathy, understanding, and connection. The sight of tears can elicit a powerful response. It can evoke empathy and compassion, compelling others to reach out, to offer a comforting word, a gentle touch, or a listening ear. This response is a testament to our capacity for empathy, our ability to understand and share the feelings of others.

So, the next time you see someone in tears, remember, it's not just an expression of pain or joy, but a call for understanding, a plea for comfort, a reminder of our shared humanity.

Tears as a Sign of God's Awareness

Tears can also be viewed as a sign of God's awareness of our struggles and joys. Tears are often seen as a language that transcends words. They are a raw, unfiltered expression of our innermost feelings, a language that God understands. When words fail us, tears become our silent prayers, our unspoken pleas, and our quiet expressions of gratitude.

Tears expose our vulnerability, revealing our human frailty and need for comfort. In these moments of openness, many believe that God's awareness is most keenly felt. The divine is seen as a comforting presence, a source of solace and strength in times of sorrow, and a beacon of joy in moments of happiness. Tears can also serve as a bridge between the humanity and God. They are a physical manifestation of our emotional and spiritual state, a visible sign of our invisible feelings. In shedding tears, we acknowledge our humanity, our need for divine intervention, and our belief in a power greater than ourselves.

The belief in God's awareness of our tears brings comfort to many. It reassures us that we are not alone in our struggles, that our joys and sorrows are seen, and that our tears are understood. This divine awareness is a source of comfort and hope, a reminder of the divine presence in our lives. It's not just a drop of water, but a sign of divine awareness, a silent prayer heard by God.

Tears in the New Creation

The concept of "New Creation" in the Christian faith refers to the transformative journey of believers through the grace of Jesus Christ. Tears often symbolize repentance. They represent a heartfelt sorrow for past sins and a desire to turn away from them. This act of repentance is a crucial step towards becoming a new creation in Christ. Tears can also signify spiritual rebirth. Just as Jesus wept in the Garden of Gethsemane, believers may shed tears during their journey towards becoming a new person. These tears symbolize the pain of dying to the old self and the joy of being born again in Christ. Tears shed in the process of becoming a new creation can also reflect the overwhelming experience of God's grace. They represent the believer's response to the profound love and mercy of God, which makes the new life possible.

Tears as a Sign of the End of Death

In many religious and philosophical traditions, tears often carry profound symbolic meanings. In the

context of Christianity, tears can be seen as a sign of the end of death, a concept deeply rooted in the faith's eschatological beliefs. Tears, in their most literal sense, are a reminder of our mortality. They are shed in times of sorrow, loss, and grief - experiences that are intrinsically tied to the human condition and the inevitability of death.
However, in the Christian faith, death is not the end but a transition to a new life. The tears shed in mourning are not just for the loss of life, but also in anticipation of the resurrection. This belief is central to the Christian faith and is encapsulated in the promise of Jesus Christ's resurrection.

The Book of Revelation speaks of a new heaven and a new earth where 'God will wipe away every tear; there shall be no more death, nor sorrow, nor crying. There shall be no more pain, for the former things have passed away' (Revelation 21:4). Here, tears are directly associated with the end of death. They are seen as something that will be wiped away in the new creation, signifying the end of all things that cause pain and suffering.

In this light, tears can also be seen as a sign of hope and joy. They are shed not just in sorrow, but also in anticipation of the joy that comes with the belief in eternal life. The end of death signifies the beginning of an eternity spent in the presence of

God, a cause for rejoicing. They are a poignant reminder of the transient nature of our earthly lives and the eternal hope we hold.

The Prayer of Tears

The 'Prayer of Tears' is a potent form of communication with our Heavenly Father. It transcends words, expressing our deepest emotions and desires. So, let us embrace our tears, for they are a sacred language, a heartfelt prayer understood by God.

In the depths of despair, we often find ourselves crying out to God. In our desperation, our tears become prayers, silent pleas for divine intervention. King David exemplifies this in Psalm 69:3,
"I am worn out calling for help; my throat is parched. My eyes fail, looking for my God."

Tears can also be shed in a fervent plea for revival, both personal and communal. Our tears, in this case, are an earnest request for spiritual rejuvenation. As in Psalm 85:6,
"Will you not revive us again, that your people may rejoice in you?"

Tears shed in brokenness are a testament to our humility and recognition of our need for God's grace. Psalm 51:17 says,

"The sacrifices of God are a broken spirit; a broken and contrite heart, O God, you will not despise." In our brokenness, our tear-filled prayers are a powerful expression of repentance and surrender.

When we are led by the Holy Spirit, our tears become a conduit for divine communication, transcending the barriers of human language. Romans 8:26 tells us,
"In the same way, the Spirit helps us in our weakness. We do not know what we ought to pray for, but the Spirit himself intercedes for us through wordless groans."

Conclusion

Why Do Humans Cry?

Crying is a multifaceted behaviour with various theories explaining its occurrence. It's a natural response to a range of emotions and serves several purposes, from physiological to psychological. Understanding why we cry can help us better understand ourselves and our emotional responses. Tears, a universal human experience, are a unique aspect of our emotional lives. But why do humans cry? This question has puzzled scientists for centuries. The act of crying is a complex process involving various physiological and psychological components.

Physiological Aspects of Crying

Tears are produced by the lacrimal glands located near the outer part of the upper eye. They serve several functions, including lubricating the eyes and removing irritants. However, emotional tears, the ones shed during moments of intense feelings, are different from basal or reflex tears. They contain more proteins and hormones, which some scientists believe are released during stressful situations.

Theories Behind Emotional Crying

Catharsis Theory: This theory suggests that crying serves as an outlet for pent-up emotions. It's a self-soothing behaviour that helps individuals cope with emotional stress.
Attachment Theory: Crying can be a non-verbal signal for help or comfort. In infants, crying is a crucial communication tool that ensures survival by signalling caregivers.
Biochemical Theory: Crying might have a biochemical purpose. The act of crying could release excess hormones or toxins from the body, helping individuals feel better.

Crying and Society
Cultural norms and societal expectations play a significant role in crying. Gender stereotypes often discourage crying, especially among males. However, crying isn't a sign of weakness but a natural emotional response that needs no shame.

Crying and Mental Health
Crying can be therapeutic. It's associated with relief, mood improvement, and stress relief. However, excessive crying could indicate underlying mental health issues, such as depression or anxiety.

The Power of Tears: An Emotional Release

Tears, often seen as a sign of vulnerability, hold immense power. They are a universal language, transcending cultural and linguistic barriers. This essay explores the power of tears, their role in emotional expression, and their impact on human connection.

Emotional Catharsis: Tears serve as an outlet for pent-up emotions. Whether it's grief, joy, frustration, or relief, crying can provide a sense of release and relief. It's a natural response that allows us to process our feelings and regain emotional equilibrium.

Communication: Tears can communicate what words often cannot. They express deep emotions and can elicit empathy and understanding from others. A tear shed in sadness can draw comfort, while tears of joy can spread happiness.

Healing: Research suggests that crying can have therapeutic effects. It can lower stress levels, improve mood, and even alleviate pain. Tears shed due to emotional stress contain certain chemicals, and releasing these chemicals through crying can promote healing.

Human Connection: Shared tears can strengthen bonds between individuals. They foster a sense of shared experience and mutual understanding, bringing people closer together.

Self-awareness: Crying also promotes self-awareness. It forces us to confront our feelings and understand what triggers our emotional responses. This self awareness can lead to personal growth and emotional resilience.

The power of tears extends beyond mere emotional expression. They are a tool for communication, a catalyst for healing, a bond of shared humanity, and a path to self-awareness. So, the next time tears well up in your eyes, remember the power they hold and let them flow. They are not a sign of weakness, but a testament to the strength of human emotion.

Additional copies of this book and other book titles from HENRY OHAKAH are available at most bookshops and from amazon.

For a complete list of titles please email us at:
henryohakah@gmail.com
henryohakah@icloud.com

Spirit Wind
Books

Bringing the healing word…touching a dying world!

Other Exciting Books

From Henry Ohakah

Come, Holy Spirit

ISBN:978-34650-0-7

Experience the Holy Spirit as never before in this captivating book about the person and work of the Holy Spirit. You will learn ways that God leads and ways that He doesn't.

Disturb Us, Lord!
ISBN:9781073518968

Too many churches have a 'Do not disturb' sign hanging on their door. May we be shaken out of our state of slumber and be jolted out of apathetic complacency.

Footsteps of Giants
ISBN: 9781725199170

There are powerful lessons to be learnt from great achievers and successful people in every walk of life, more importantly the giants of the Christian faith. Truth is that they were not lazy, dull, inactive, or idle. They inherited the promises not by wishful thinking but by careful observation and planning.

Retake Your Safe Space Let me be honest with you; It is unavoidable that some people are going to be better than you at some things where they spend the most time practicing or where they have a natural talent. But do you know that sometimes these people neglect other areas of life where you are better than they are? You are not inferior, you are not superior, you are simply you. Your value comes from your uniqueness. Never, ever compare yourself with anyone. Other people are nervous too! My advice would be to care more about what you think of yourself. Get rooted in your own value system. Stop changing or bending yourself depending on who is around. A "grasshopper mentality" prevents you from viewing yourself through your own area of strength and that's why I said other people might be nervous.

Be Yourself During Change: Preserving Self-identity Through Life's Shifts

Tears in a bottle is a profound narrative inspired by Psalm 56:8. It traces the Christian's journey through sorrow, symbolizing their tears as collected in God's bottle. The book beautifully illustrates the transformative power of grief, emphasizing that each tear is a testament to resilience and healing.

About the Author

Henry has a background in accounting and finance. He is a cultural architect and a social justice activist. Henry seeks to bring the Gospel of Jesus Christ to people irrespective of their background and experiences, leaving his accounting profession to respond to God's call of "bringing the healing word and touching a dying world" (Matthew 10:7-8). He is a sought-after conference speaker and crusade evangelist and has spoken at churches and large outdoor gospel campaigns in cities across Europe, Africa, and the USA. Henry releases the glory and power of God everywhere he goes with a strong prophetic anointing with deep insights into the Word of God that motivates you to be successful and rapturable.

Henry is a unique breed Methodist minister who is serving the Lord as a "reverse" missionary in the United Kingdom and president/founder of Spirit Wind World Impact. In his spare time, he enjoys football, writing and jumping around with his children.

Spirit Wind
WORLD IMPACT
CONNECT WITH US ON
S♥cial Medi@
@henrycohakah
@doccharismata
Henry C Ohakah
@doccharismata

SUBSCRIBE
To my
You Tube
CHANNEL
Spirit Wind
with Henry C. Ohakah
AND PRESS THE
NOTIFICATION
BATTON TO GET ALERT
AFTER EVERY UPLOAD
HENRYOHAKAH@ICLOUD.COM
WWW.SPIRITWINDWORLDIMPACT.COM

00:00
FOLLOW ME ON
TikTok
@doccharismata

Invite Henry to Speak at Your Church or Event

Inviting Rev Henry to come and minister is simple. We work with churches and ministries of all sizes. Henry has preached the Word both locally in England and across the world in places like the USA, Switzerland, and Nigeria, and has conducted open-air gospel campaigns in Togo, Benin Republic, Cameroon, Liberia, and Nigeria. Please let us have these details when you write in. You are under no obligation to book, and the invitation is finalized and scheduled only when the event is confirmed.

Your name and title/position at your church/ministry, email, best phone number to reach you at, name of the church/ministry hosting the event, event location/address, dates & times you want Henry to minister.

Contact Information

EUROPE
Spirit Wind World Impact
#61 School Drive
READING, RG5 3PZ
UNITED KINGDOM
Phone: +44-118-4374-895
Email : henryohakah@icloud.com
Website: henryohakah.wixsite.com/swwi
https://youtube.com/@spiritwindwithhenry

AFRICA
Henry Ohakah Foundation
54 Cameroun Road, PO Box 2721
UMUAHIA, NIGERIA
Phone : +234-802-451-1616
Email : henryohakah@gmail.com

Notes

Notes

Printed in Great Britain
by Amazon

44068858R00066